Numbats

Victoria Blakemore

Table of Contents

What Are Numbats?

Numbats are small mammals.

They are a special kind of

mammal called a **marsupial**.

They are different from most

mammals because their

babies are born **undeveloped**.

The babies are carried on the

mother's body while they are

still growing.

2

Numbats are a mix of different

colors. They are red-orange,

brown, gray, white, and black.

Size

Numbats are small animals. They often grow to be less than ten inches long. Their tail adds another fix or six inches to their length.

Since they are so small, they do not weigh much. Most numbats weigh less than one and a half pounds.

Male numbats are usually a bit

heavier than female numbats.

Physical Characteristics

Numbats have a long, pointy **snout**. It helps them dig into the dirt to look for food.

They have claws on their feet. They are not very strong, but they can be used to dig in the dirt to get the termites they eat.

Numbats use **camouflage** to
hide from their **predators**. Their
stripes help them blend in with
their habitat.

Habitat

Numbats used to live in grasslands, woodlands, and eucalyptus forests. Now, they are found mainly in eucalyptus forests.

They live in areas with lots of fallen logs because they use them to find food and sleep in at night.

Range

Numbats are only found in parts of Australia.

They live in the western parts of

Australia, mainly in the south.

Diet

Unlike other **marsupials**, numbats are **insectivores**. They only eat insects.

Their diet is almost completely made up of termites. They have been known to eat around 20,000 termites each day.

Termites are insects that live in

logs and under the ground. They

are usually smaller than one inch

in length.

Numbats have a long, sticky tongue. They use their tongue to catch termites by sticking it into holes in logs and the dirt. The termites stick to their tongue and the numbat eats them.

Numbats do not drink much water. They get most of their water from the termites they eat.

Numbats have a long tongue for such a small animal. It can be over four inches long.

Communication

Numbats use mainly sound and scent to communicate. While they are usually **solitary**, numbats use clicking sounds when they are around other numbats.

They may also growl or hiss as a warning if another animal gets too close.

Male numbats make a special oil that they use to rub on trees and rocks. It tells other numbats to stay away from their **territory**.

Movement

Numbats can run at speeds of up to about 20 miles per hour. They need to be quick to escape to their den if a **predator** is chasing them.

They are good at climbing and use their sharp claws to climb trees when they are looking for food.

Numbats spend a lot of their time walking around with their nose to the ground. They do this to smell for food.

Numbat Joeys

Numbats usually have four babies, or **joeys**. They are born very tiny and must hold on to their mother until they are about nine months old.

The mother feeds them milk for the first nine months, then they are able to start eating termites.

Numbats stay with their mothers until they are about one year old. Then, they leave to find their own **territory**.

Numbat Life

Numbats are **diurnal**. They are most active during the day. This is different from most **marsupials**, which are most active at night.

When it is cold, they come out for a few hours when the sun is up and it is warmest. When it is hot, they rest in the shade during the hottest parts of the day.

At night, numbats sleep in hollow logs, holes in trees, or in burrows they dig in the dirt.

Banded Anteaters

Numbats are also known as banded anteaters. They are called this because they have similar **characteristics** to anteaters.

While they have a long tongue for eating insects and a long snout, numbats are not closely related to anteaters.

Anteaters are not **marsupials**

like numbats.

Population

Numbats are **endangered**. There are not many left in the wild. There are thought to be less than 1,000 numbats left in the wild.

If numbat populations continue to **decline**, they may become **extinct**.

Numbats often live about five years in the wild. They have been known to live up to eight years.

Numbats in Danger

Numbats are facing several threats. They are often hunted by animals such as foxes, snakes, and **feral** cats.

Another threat to numbats is habitat loss. They have fewer safe places to live now than they used to.

Numbat habitats have been

cleared for buildings, roads,

mining, and farming.

Helping Numbats

People are working to help numbats so that they do not become **extinct**.

There are special **preserves** set up to provide animals like numbats with a safe place to live. Almost all wild numbats live in these protected areas.

30

The Perth Zoo in Australia is one organization that is working to help wild numbats. They breed numbats that are then released into the wildlife preserves.

Their goal is to help wild numbat populations to grow so that they will continue to live in the wild.

Glossary

Camouflage: using color to blend in to the surroundings

Carnivore: an animal that eats only meat

Characteristics: something that can make a person or animal different from others

Decline: to get smaller

Diurnal: most active during the day

Endangered: at risk of becoming extinct

Extinct: when there are no more of an animal left in the wild

Feral: a wild animal, not a pet

Insectivore: an animal that eats only insects

Joey: a baby marsupial

Marsupial: a kind of mammal whose babies are born undeveloped and must stay in a pouch or on the mother's body while they are growing

Predator: an animal that hunts other animals for food

Preserves: areas of land set up to protect plants and animals

Snout: an animal's nose and mouth

Solitary: living alone

Territory: an area of land that an animal claims as its own

Undeveloped: not fully grown

About the Author

Victoria Blakemore is a first grade

teacher in Southwest Florida with a

passion for reading.

You can visit her at

www.elementaryexplorers.com

Also in This Series

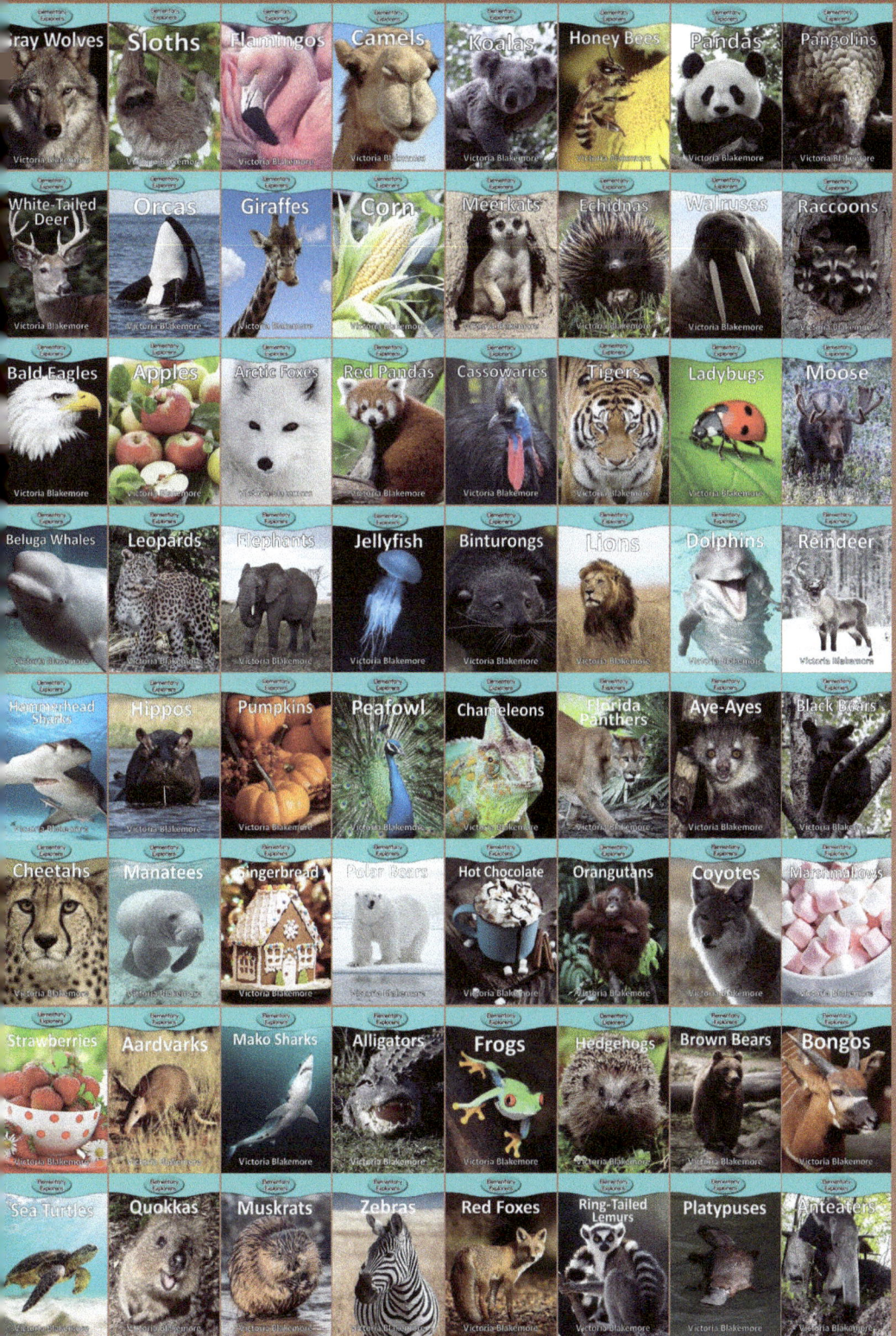

Gray Wolves | Sloths | Flamingos | Camels | Koalas | Honey Bees | Pandas | Pangolins

White-Tailed Deer | Orcas | Giraffes | Corn | Meerkats | Echidnas | Walruses | Raccoons

Bald Eagles | Apples | Arctic Foxes | Red Pandas | Cassowaries | Tigers | Ladybugs | Moose

Beluga Whales | Leopards | Elephants | Jellyfish | Binturongs | Lions | Dolphins | Reindeer

Hammerhead Sharks | Hippos | Pumpkins | Peafowl | Chameleons | Florida Panthers | Aye-Ayes | Black Bears

Cheetahs | Manatees | Gingerbread | Polar Bears | Hot Chocolate | Orangutans | Coyotes | Marshmallows

Strawberries | Aardvarks | Mako Sharks | Alligators | Frogs | Hedgehogs | Brown Bears | Bongos

Sea Turtles | Quokkas | Muskrats | Zebras | Red Foxes | Ring-Tailed Lemurs | Platypuses | Anteaters

Also in This Series

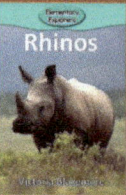

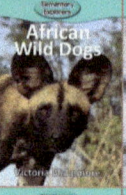

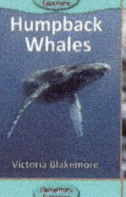

Kangaroos · Rhinos · Jaguars · Wombats · Capybaras · Gorillas · Cats · Skunks

Butterflies · Dingoes · Snow Leopards · African Wild Dogs · Penguins · Whale Sharks · Wolverines · Warthogs

Caracals · Badgers · Seals · Hummingbirds · Pikas · Humpback Whales · Pumas · Lemonade

Llamas · Tulips · Ostriches · Sunflowers · Fennec Foxes · Sea Lions · Squirrels · Roses

Porcupines · Ice Cream · Cotton Candy · Chocolate · Hyenas · Toucans · Saigas · Puffins

Doughnuts · Dholes · Kudus · Ocelots · Numbats

www.ingramcontent.com/pod-product-compliance
Lightning Source LLC
Chambersburg PA
CBHW052124030426
42335CB00025B/3111